Looking *at* Pictures

Telling a Story

~ Joy Richardson ~

W

FRANKLIN WATTS

LONDON•SYDNEY

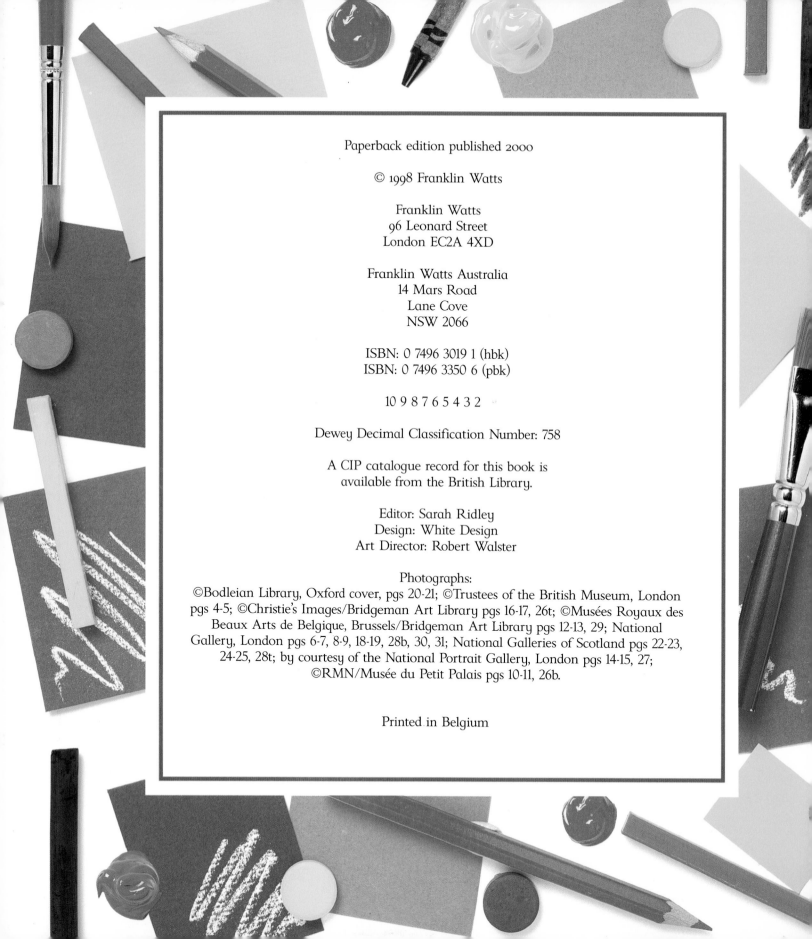

Paperback edition published 2000

© 1998 Franklin Watts

Franklin Watts
96 Leonard Street
London EC2A 4XD

Franklin Watts Australia
14 Mars Road
Lane Cove
NSW 2066

ISBN: 0 7496 3019 1 (hbk)
ISBN: 0 7496 3350 6 (pbk)

10 9 8 7 6 5 4 3 2

Dewey Decimal Classification Number: 758

A CIP catalogue record for this book is
available from the British Library.

Editor: Sarah Ridley
Design: White Design
Art Director: Robert Walster

Printed in Belgium

Contents

How do you tell a story in a single picture?

Explore the pictures in this book to enjoy some stories told by artists.

A Scene from the Book of the Dead of Anhai 4
The Legend of the Wolf of Gubbio 6
Saint George and the Dragon 8
Theseus and the Minotaur 10
Fall of Icarus 12
Sir Henry Unton 14
The Animals Entering the Ark 16
Belshazzar's Feast 18
An Episode from The Thousand and One Nights 20
The Quarrel of Oberon and Titania 22
The Pied Piper of Hamelin 24
Story Telling in Paint 26
More about the pictures in this book 30
Index 32

A Scene from the Book of the Dead of Anhai

painted by an Egyptian artist

This story picture was put in a tomb
to form part of a guide to the land of the dead.

A boat sails on the River Nile.

Reeds grow tall and are ready for cutting.

Oxen plough the land.

The Legend of the Wolf of Gubbio
painted by Sassetta

Saint Francis and the wolf agree.
It will stop attacking people, in return for food.

They shake hands on the deal.

A lawyer writes it all down.

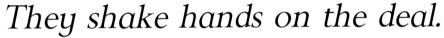

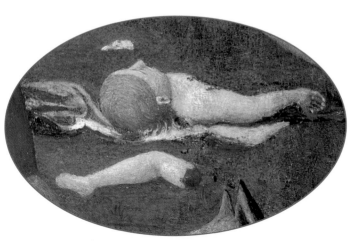

Look what the wolf has done.

No wonder people felt scared.

Saint George and the Dragon
painted by Uccello

Saint George rides in to rescue
the princess from the hungry dragon.

The horse rears.

Saint George strikes with his lance.

The dragon meets his match.

The princess looks on.

Theseus and the Minotaur
painted by the Master of the
Campana Cassoni

Theseus sails across the sea to kill
the minotaur in the maze.
Ariadne gives him thread to mark his route.

How many times can you see Theseus in the picture?

Ariadne waits for him to come back.

Theseus kills the man-bull monster.

Theseus and his friends sail safely away.

Fall of Icarus
painted by Bruegel

Icarus was trying to fly like a bird
but the sun melted the wax on his feathers.

Icarus plunges into the sea.

Sheep graze
quietly beside their
shepherd and his dog.

Ships sail on
their way.

Has anyone noticed
Icarus plunging
from the sky?

Sir Henry Unton (detail)

painted by an unknown artist

Follow the story of one man's
life from his birth to his death.

Find him in his mother's arms,

studying at university,

travelling abroad,

feasting at home,

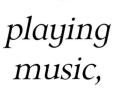

playing music,

falling ill

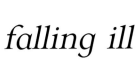

and on his way to his funeral.

The Animals Entering the Ark
painted by Savery

Noah took animals in pairs
on board his boat to save them
from the coming flood.

Birds fly round as the storm clouds gather.

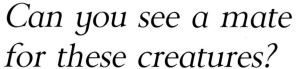

Animals head into the ark.

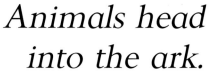

Can you see a mate for these creatures?

Belshazzar's Feast
painted by Rembrandt

What's that scary writing?
Everyone stops to stare
at the mystery marks on the wall.

The hand appears from nowhere.

The King's eyes
nearly pop out
of his head.

Wine spills.

Frightened faces
gape at the sight.

An Episode from
The Thousand and One Nights

painted by a Mughal artist

The prince saw the portrait of a magical
princess and has travelled the world to find her.

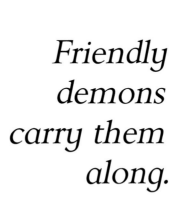

The happy prince and princess fly away together.

Friendly demons carry them along.

Winged servants float through the air in cloud carriages.

The earth below bursts into life.

The Quarrel of Oberon and Titania
painted by Paton

There is magic about on midsummer's night,
as the King and Queen of the fairies
argue over a little boy.

Fairies flutter
through the forest.

The mischievous
boy clings to Titania.

Oberon wants to
take him away.

Playful Puck
will help him.

The Pied Piper of Hamelin
painted by Christie

The Pied Piper plays his magic pipe.
All the children follow him, never to be seen again.

The Pied Piper plays
a magic tune.

It makes
the children
happy.

They follow
him through
the woods.

Baby comes too.

Story Telling in Paint

Choosing your moment

Artists often choose just one moment from a story.

Try making a picture of a different moment from one of the stories in this book.

From beginning to ending

Some pictures show several episodes from a story all rolled into one scene.

Try combining two episodes from a story to make one picture.

For help, look at pages 4, 10 and 14.

Life story

Think of five important times in your life so far.

Try putting them all into a picture to tell the story of your life.

For help, look at pages 4 and 14.

Stories in stories

Artists fill out the picture with foreground and background details.

Try telling your own story about these little scenes.

For help, look at pages 6, 12 and 22.

Story focus

A picture may lead your eye straight to the main character or event, or you may have to look hard to find it.

Try painting this story with the main event going on in the foreground.

For help, look at pages 10 and 12.

More about the pictures in this book

■ A Scene from the Book of the Dead of Anhai

These scenes were painted on papyrus in ancient Egypt around 1150 BC. They come from a Book of the Dead which was placed in a tomb as a guide to the afterlife. They show the dead man cultivating the land in the Field of Reeds, a home-from-home paradise where the dead were believed to dwell. Such scenes were created to help carry the pleasant life of ancient Egypt through into the afterlife.

■ The Legend of the Wolf of Gubbio

Stefano di Giovanni Sassetta (about 1392-1450) was an Italian painter who worked in Siena. This picture was made for the altar of a church. It was one of eight small panels showing scenes from the life of Saint Francis, a peacemaker who had a special way with animals.

■ Saint George and the Dragon

Paolo Uccello (1397-1475) lived in Florence, Italy. In this picture he shows the legend of Saint George rescuing the king's daughter, who had been chosen as the flesh-eating dragon's latest victim. Uccello shows Saint George riding to the rescue but also shows the next part of the story, with the princess already calmly holding the subdued dragon by a lead.

■ Theseus and the Minotaur

The Master of the Campana Cassoni (whose real name is unknown) made this painting around 1510. It shows the ancient Greek legend of Theseus killing the minotaur, in an up-to-date Italian setting. This picture is organised to show the whole sequence of the story at once.

■ Fall of Icarus

Pieter Bruegel the Elder (about 1515-1569) was a Dutch painter. Daedalus and his son Icarus escaped from Crete on wings made from feathers fixed with wax. Icarus flew too close to the sun, the wax melted and the wings fell apart. Bruegel shows life going on as usual, as Icarus disappears into the sea.

■ Sir Henry Unton

An unknown artist painted this picture around 1596. The main events of Unton's life are shown anti-clockwise from the bottom right, and his life at home is illustrated in the middle. The story continues onto the left half of the picture (not shown here) with Unton's funeral and a portrait of him.

The Animals Entering the Ark

Jacob II Savery (1593-1627) was a Dutch painter. This picture tells the story of Noah's Ark from the book of Genesis in the Bible. God told Noah to build a giant boat so that when the coming rain flooded the earth, his family and two animals of each kind would be saved.

Belshazzar's Feast

Rembrandt (1606-1669) was a Dutch painter. Here he captures a dramatic moment from a Bible story. Writing appeared mysteriously on the wall, interrupting King Belshazzar's feast. Only Daniel, a Jewish servant, could read what it said: the King, who had taken gold and silver from the temple in Jerusalem, was to be punished. Enemies attacked that night, and King Belshazzar died.

An Episode from The Thousand and One Nights

This picture was made around 1760, by a Mughal artist. It illustrates the amazing tale of the Egyptian Prince Saif ul-Muluk, who had many adventures in his quest for Badi'al-Jamal. She was a princess of the Jinn, superhuman beings who appear in many forms. The story comes from the great Arabic collection 'The Thousand and One Nights'.

The Quarrel of Oberon and Titania

Sir Joseph Noel Paton (1821-1901) lived in Scotland. This picture illustrates a scene from William Shakespeare's play 'A Midsummer Night's Dream'. Puck helps to make magic so that Titania falls in love with whomever she first sees on waking. The forest is full of fairy creatures on this most magical night of the year.

The Pied Piper of Hamelin

James Elder Christie (1847-1914) was a Scottish painter. The Pied Piper of Hamelin is a German legend from the thirteenth century. The Pied Piper rid Hamelin of a plague of rats. When he was not paid he played his magic pipe again. All the children followed him out of the city, never to return.

Index

animals 16, 17, 30, 31
Ariadne 10, 11
ark 16, 17, 31

Belshazzar 18, 31
Book of the Dead 4, 30
Bruegel 12, 30

children 24, 25, 31
Christie 24, 31

demons 21
dragon 8, 9, 30

Egyptian artist 4

fairies 22, 23, 31

Icarus 12, 13, 30

King 19, 22, 30, 31

Master of the Campana
   Cassoni 10, 30
minotaur 10, 30
Mughal artist 20

Noah 16, 31

Oberon 22, 23, 31

Paton 22, 31
Pied Piper 24, 25, 31
prince 20, 21, 31
princess 8, 9, 20, 21, 30, 31

Queen 22

Rembrandt 18, 31

Saint Francis 6, 30
Saint George 8, 9, 30
Sassetta 6, 30
Savery 16, 30
Sir Henry Unton 14, 30

Theseus 10, 11, 30
The Thousand and One
   Nights 20, 31
Titania 22, 23, 31

Uccello 8, 30

wolf 6, 7, 30